Our Neighbors

CHINESE AMERICANS

by Elizabeth Andrews

DiscoverRoo
An Imprint of Pop!
popbooksonline.com

abdobooks.com

Published by Pop!, a division of ABDO, PO Box 398166, Minneapolis, Minnesota 55439.

Printed in the United States of America, North Mankato, Minnesota.

052021
092021

THIS BOOK CONTAINS RECYCLED MATERIALS

Cover Photos: Shutterstock Images

Interior Photos: Shutterstock Images, 1, 13, 20–21, 26; iStockphoto, 5, 8, 11, 17, 18, 22 (bottom), 25, 28; Mihai_Andritoiu/Shutterstock.com, 6; PF-(usna)/Alamy, 14; Historical/Shutterstock, 22 (top); Uncredited/AP/Shutterstock, 23 (top); Allen J Schaben/Los Angeles Times/Shutterstock, 23 (bottom)

Editor: Tyler Gieseke
Series Designer: Laura Graphenteen

Library of Congress Control Number: 2020948916

Publisher's Cataloging-in-Publication Data

Names: Andrews, Elizabeth, author.

Title: Chinese Americans / by Elizabeth Andrews

Description: Minneapolis, Minnesota : Pop!, 2022 | Series: Our neighbors | Includes online resources and index.

Identifiers: ISBN 9781098240028 (lib. bdg.) | ISBN 9781644945964 (pbk.) | ISBN 9781098240943 (ebook)

Subjects: LCSH: Chinese Americans--Juvenile literature. | Ethnicity--United States--Juvenile literature. | Neighbors--Juvenile literature. | Immigrants--United States--History--Juvenile literature.

Classification: DDC 973.004--dc23

WELCOME TO DiscoverRoo!

Pop open this book and you'll find QR codes loaded with information, so you can learn even more!

Scan this code* and others like it while you read, or visit the website below to make this book pop!

popbooksonline.com/chinese-americans

*Scanning QR codes requires a web-enabled smart device with a QR code reader app and a camera.

TABLE OF CONTENTS

CHAPTER 1

A SPECIAL TRADITION

Peter helped his mother sweep the floor of their kitchen. They had been cleaning all morning. He knew it would continue into the afternoon. After everything was

WATCH A VIDEO HERE!

Red means joy, luck, and happiness in Chinese culture.

spick-and-span, they hung red banners on their walls and put red lanterns in their windows and doors.

It was Lunar New Year's Eve. His family looked forward to this day all year. It wasn't the same New Year his friends from school celebrated on January 1. Lunar New Year was different and even more special to him.

The longer the dragon is, the more luck it will bring to communities.

Peter and his family are Chinese American. This is their most important holiday. Lunar New Year is a time to start fresh and think of good things to come. It usually is early in February, but the date changes with the **moon cycle**.

LUNAR NEW YEAR FESTIVAL

At the Lunar New Year's festival in San Francisco, a 288-foot (87.8 m) dragon is carried through the streets during a parade. The dragon is called *Gum Lung*. It takes 180 people to carry it. They move in patterns together so it looks like the dragon is dancing. The head of the dragon weighs 30 pounds (13.6 kg)!

The Lantern Festival marks the end of Lunar New Year festivities.

Peter and his family clean the house to get all the bad luck out before celebrations start. Soon his grandparents will be over. They will share a yummy meal of fish and dumplings. In the morning Peter will get to open the red envelopes waiting for him.

DID YOU KNOW?

Red envelopes are a Lunar New Year tradition. They are usually filled with gifts of money!

CHAPTER 2

HOMELAND

In the early 1800s, it was normal for Chinese laborers to leave their home and work in other countries. China had high taxes after a war that had already forced workers off their land. China was

LEARN MORE HERE!

facing **economic** troubles. These issues pushed Chinese people to look elsewhere for jobs.

Some years, Chinese farmers produce one-third of the world's rice.

People from China started coming to America around 1850. America was a land full of opportunities. The **California Gold Rush** began in 1848 and pulled in many men from China. They would send their money back to their families. Taking care of family was a big reason for Chinese **immigration**.

DID YOU KNOW?

The Gold Rush brought 25,000 Chinese immigrants to the United States.

CHINESE IMMIGRATION

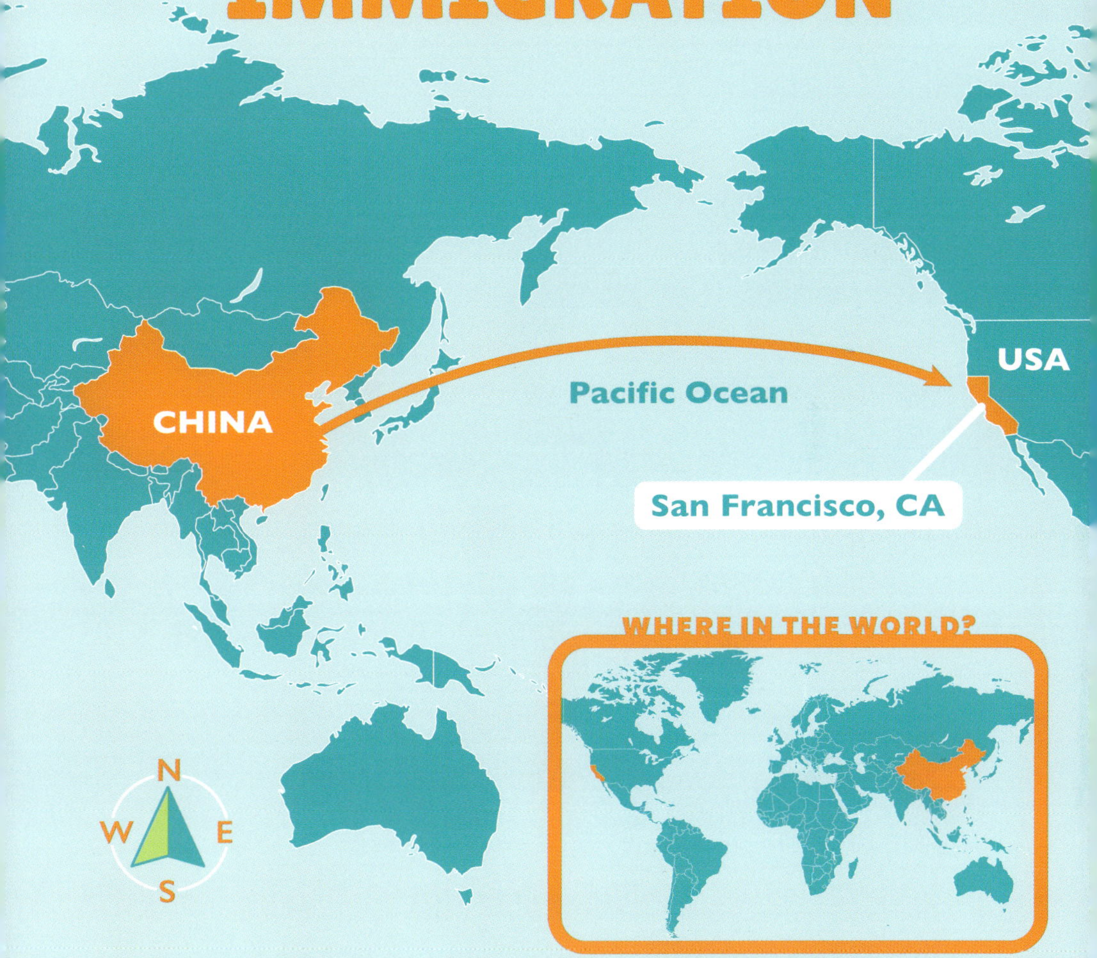

The trip from China to America was fastest over the Pacific Ocean. It took three weeks by ship. This path brought them to the West Coast. When the Gold Rush started, Chinese people could get to California easily.

Sometimes whole families moved to the United States when the father came to work.

America held a promising future for laborers. But, the Chinese faced **discrimination** when they arrived. Americans sometimes wrongly thought Chinese immigrants were criminals. The government even stopped letting Chinese people move to the United States in 1882. This lasted until China and America became **allies** in 1943 during World War II. After that, the United States welcomed Chinese immigrants again.

CHAPTER 3

BUILDING A LIFE

Chinese Americans make up the third-largest **immigrant** group in the United States. The first Chinese immigrants settled along the West Coast. They often chose California. Today, Chinese Americans live all over the country.

COMPLETE AN ACTIVITY HERE!

Chinese American families have many reasons to be happy in the United States!

Families feel a lot of pride when they watch younger generations grow and succeed.

Family is very important to Chinese Americans. Grandparents may offer to watch the kids. Sometimes, they even live with their family to help out. They see it as an honor. Children spend a lot of time growing close with their grandparents. Chinese values easily spread to the youngest generation. Parents work hard to give their kids and the older generation a happy life.

DID YOU KNOW?

A traditional Chinese meal will always contain rice.

The children of Chinese Americans often speak both English and Mandarin. They will speak Mandarin with the older

American schools teach children from all different kinds of backgrounds!

members of their family when at home. At school, they will speak in English with their teachers and friends.

CHINESE IMMIGRATION TIMELINE

1842

The first Opium War ends. Many Chinese people have been forced off their land. They are looking for work.

1848

The **California Gold Rush** begins. Chinese laborers move to the United States looking for work.

1882

America stops letting people **immigrate** from China.

A woman flies a Chinese flag on a Miami beach.

1943

America and China have an **alliance**. America begins allowing Chinese people to immigrate again.

1964

The **discrimination** Chinese Americans face eases. They begin to mix into American society.

2019

Chinese Americans begin facing discrimination again after an illness called COVID-19 spreads from China.

CHAPTER 4

A WONDERFUL MIX

Chinese parents believe America can give their children a bright future. It's important to them that their children make use of every opportunity they get, including education.

LEARN MORE HERE!

Graduating is an exciting accomplishment for any student!

Children of **immigrant** families often try to balance their two **cultures**. Chinese Americans might act one way with their family and another way with their friends. They will start to **adapt** parts of American and Chinese cultures and become a wonderful blend of both. Chinese American kids might work very hard at school like their parents want. They may also share the independent attitude of their American peers.

At school, Chinese American kids may work hard in class and at sports.

Chinatowns are filled with all kinds of Chinese culture, like food and art!

Since they first arrived in the 1850s, Chinese Americans have built what are now known as Chinatowns.

These communities mix both American and Chinese cultures. Chinatowns offer traditional meals and have classic Chinese buildings. You can hear Chinese languages spoken around every corner. Often, older and younger generations are seen enjoying the taste of their homeland. These communities show what it means to be Chinese American.

DID YOU KNOW?

There are more than 50 busy Chinatowns in cities around the United States.

MAKING CONNECTIONS

TEXT-TO-SELF

Young Chinese kids are often close to their grandparents. Are you close with your grandparents? If not, do you wish you were?

TEXT-TO-TEXT

Have you read other books about immigrants in America? What do they have in common with this title? How are they different?

TEXT-TO-WORLD

Chinese immigrants were treated better after the 1940s. Can you think about other groups of people who were treated differently over time?

GLOSSARY

adapt — to change behaviors to better fit conditions.

ally — a country that has partnered with another for a particular purpose.

California Gold Rush — (1848-1855) a time when thousands of people from around the world traveled to Northern California after gold had been found at Stutter's Mill.

culture — the arts, beliefs, and ways of life of a group of people.

discrimination — unfair treatment, often based on race, religion, or gender.

economic — related to how goods and services are made, sold, and used.

immigrate — to enter another country to live. A person who immigrates is an immigrant.

moon cycle — the phases of the moon as it travels around the Earth.

INDEX

ONLINE RESOURCES

popbooksonline.com

Scan this code* and others like it while you read, or visit the website below to make this book pop!

popbooksonline.com/chinese-americans

*Scanning QR codes requires a web-enabled smart device with a QR code reader app and a camera.